The wheel garden

garden

Story by Annette Smith
Illustrations by Margaret Power

2

One day, after school,
James went to play at Scott's house
for the first time.

"I want to have a garden like yours,"
said Scott.
"But we don't have any room."

"Do you have a wheelbarrow?" said James.

"A wheelbarrow!" said Scott. "No, we don't have one."

"You can make a little garden in a wheelbarrow," said James.

Scott's mother came out.

James said to her, "We have
an old wheelbarrow at home.
I will see if Scott can have it."

"Then I can make a little garden
in it," smiled Scott.

On Saturday, James and his dad
came over to Scott's house,
with the old wheelbarrow.

"Here's the wheelbarrow," said James,
"and here are some peas
to plant in your garden."

The boys pushed the wheelbarrow
down the path.
They put it by the fence in the sun.

"Look at all the things
we got from the garden shop
this morning," Scott said to James.

Scott's dad helped the boys.

"You can put the stones and sand

in first," he said.

"I will get the bags of potting soil."

"Here are some little plants,"

said Scott's mother.

"I will show you what to do," said James.

The boys worked all morning. They put in some sticks for the peas to climb up. They planted all the things from the pots.

"Thanks, James," said Scott.

"Now I have a garden, too."